This book is a must-read if...

- you want to understand yourself

- you wish to discover more about how you think

- you wish to build a positive, growth mindset

- you want to stop doubting yourself

- you want to achieve every goal you set in life

- you want to learn to be UNSTOPPABLE!

I was so impressed with Onkaar and Avneet's assertiveness in their book *Everyday Mindset.* They have proved to be young thought leaders.

This book gives you powerful hints and tips on how to be in control, stop doubting ourselves and believe that we can achieve anything we put our mind to.

Every child and adult should read this book.

Andrea Malam BEM
Charity Founder and Trustee, Author, Speaker, Philanthropist
and Humanitarian

"Nobody can add time to your LIFE,
But we can add LIFE to our TIME"

This is what I can say regarding Onkaar and Avneet's book. They are giving LIFE to the ATTITUDE which every one must REFLECT in their life. I am shocked with the incredible thoughts, passion and dedication of these two Budding Stars. It's inspiring and innovative.

Wishing JOURNEY OF EXCELLENCE to both the STARS.

Dr Shama Hussain
Founder, Director and Global CEO, International Institute of Influencers
Country Director, United Nations Peace Keepers Federation Council

This book by Onkaar and Avneet is a great all-round mindset workbook that is broken down in ways that helps children and even adults.

They have touched on many key areas, such as name, and identity, goal setting, affirmations and even dealing with personal emotions, as well as helping those around us navigate theirs.

I recommend this book to all parents as a great practical introduction to mindset and acquiring lifelong skills in this area to set them up for success.

Ihuaku Patricia Nweke, BSc, MSc, MCIPS
Founder and CEO of Cedarcube
Founder and Chair of International Consortium for Domestic Peace
Director of I.Kollection fashion

I love this book. There are wonderful quotations to support each chapter and the fact that the book is written by children for children is what makes it stand out.

It is a great book for young people to help them to feel good about themselves and use the techniques and advice offered in the book. Onkaar and Avneet are great role models to any other aspiring authors.

Lisa Bedlow
Founder of Gabriels Wellbeing & Education

Hello! We are Onkaar and Avneet and we are award-winning, bestselling authors. We have written self-help books for young people. Our aim is to empower young people as their minds and bodies GROW.

We have each won awards for our writing and actively teaching young people in workshops about Confidence, Mindset, Healthy Lifestyles and Nature.

It has taken us a lot of work to get this far, and we have learnt so much on our journey. But the most important thing for us has been to remember that our VOICE IS VALUABLE! And so is yours!

Your voice is unique and powerful. As young people, we have a unique perspective on the world, life and even on ourselves. Our mind absorbs things very quickly. The skills we teach ourselves now will serve us well in the future. So use this book to train yourself now... after all, we are the FUTURE!

We want to help and encourage you to believe in yourself and have the right mindset to take on everything life will throw at you.

In this book, you will learn more about yourself and use the activities to learn techniques to enable a powerful mindset and other life skills which will aid you going forward.

LIFE SKILLS
TOOLBOX

"Your mind is your most powerful tool. Take control and discover the power inside you!"

Onkaar & Avneet

Acknowledgements

We want to thank our parents and teachers. They have always helped us to explore and learn new lessons on our journey through life. We call it the 'Game of Life' and we are here to enjoy it!

We also want to thank each other for being brilliant companions as brother and sister. Sometimes we bicker but we always make each other think about the bigger picture and we value the important things in life.

We want to give special thanks to Brenda Dempsey, CEO and Founder of Book Brilliance Publishing. We are working hard together to help young people grow and shine.

We hope you enjoy this book!

Onkaar & Avneet

To our family and friends
… and anyone
who wants to GROW!

"Once your mindset changes, everything on the outside will change along with it."

Steve Maraboli
motivational speaker and author

Everyday
Mindset

ONKAAR & AVNEET NIJJER

First published in Great Britain in 2023
by Spark of Brilliance
an imprint of Book Brilliance Publishing
265A Fir Tree Road, Epsom, Surrey, KT17 3LF
+44 (0)20 8641 5090
www.bookbrilliancepublishing.com
admin@bookbrilliancepublishing.com

A CIP catalogue record for this book is available at the British Library.

ISBN 978-1-913770-57-0

Typeset in Helvetica.

Contents

Foreword

Yet another book from two fantastic young people who know exactly what it takes to make a success of themselves and how to inspire others. This book tells us how the mechanics of a growth mindset really work and what children and parents 'need to do' so as to cultivate a mindset that keeps you feeling good, able to reach one's goals and thrive through difficulty and challenge.

Today's children and young people face many academic pressures, mental health struggles, societal and other pressures which can mean it feels harder to keep striving and feeling positive. They require genuine and evidence-based tools that they can 'try and apply' in different scenarios.

One of the great assets of this book is that children are modelling to other children which tools work and why. The authors define, in clear and accessible language, what a growth mindset is, how it differs from a 'fixed mindset', and how it optimises a child's chance of thriving in all aspects of their life. They also showcase real-life role models who have been able to thrive through failure and who see mistakes as part of learning.

My favourite aspect of the book is that these siblings co-created this creative book. If families are able to develop a growth mindset together, it is optimal; they can motivate one another to stay on track, support each other along the way and use the language of growth mindset in everyday conversation. If children struggle, we need to suggest they can't do it 'yet'. If they fail, it is the first attempt at learning. If they do well, we can praise their perseverance rather than their performance. Language matters, attitude and mindset all come together to give children an optimal chance to thrive.

The power of this book is that it gives children agency to affect change in their lives and control where they might feel out of control. It is a genuine and age-appropriate handbook that can inspire pupils in the classroom, children at home and even the adults that work with or care for them every day.

Dr Kathy Weston
Founder, Tooled Up Education

CHAPTER 1

INTRODUCTION

"We may have all come on different ships, but we're in the same boat now."

Martin Luther King Jr.
civil rights activist

You are not alone

There are over seven billion people in the world!

Correct! You are definitely not alone!

But have you ever wondered:

Does anyone else feel the way I feel?

You might sometimes feel unsure about what to do, or you might feel worried about how to do something.

That is okay.

In fact, it is good because, while growing up, you want to feel a range of emotions. This is because we learn and grow by experiencing different things.

But sometimes if you have some feelings too often, like doubting yourself or telling yourself that you cannot do something, then it can start to hold you back.

This book will give you lots of hints and tips about how to be in control of your mind and be on top of your game! Yes, the GAME OF LIFE!

Famous people and their mindsets

Famous people have had many years of practice to master what they do.

Interestingly, they have also had many years to work on their mindset which makes them stronger and better at achieving their success.

In fact, their mind is their most powerful tool and their mindset is the foundation of how to achieve their goals and dreams!

Remember, success does not just happen overnight.

"Failure is so important.

We speak about success
all the time.

It is the ability to use failure
that often leads to
greater success."

J.K. Rowling
author of the Harry Potter books and others

The famous author J. K. Rowling took seven years to write the first Harry Potter novel.

The manuscript was rejected by all of the major publishers.

But she believed in herself and her work to make it a success.

"In the middle of difficulty
lies opportunity."

Albert Einstein
theoretical physicist

$E = mc^2$

Albert Einstein is famous for being a genius.

BUT even he found some things difficult!

However, he would not let that stop him.

In fact, his mindset would allow him to see any difficulty or challenge as an opportunity.

When our mind sees an opportunity, it releases positive energy and is happy. So when Einstein looked at something difficult or challenging, his positive mindset would allow him to find a solution.

POSITIVE ENERGY = POSITIVE RESULTS

"I can accept failure,
everyone fails at something.

But I can't accept not trying."

Michael Jordan
basketball player and businessman

Michael Jordan is the GREATEST basketball player of all time.

In order to be a great sportsperson, it takes a powerful mind to have the required discipline and resilience.

Jordan did not win every game he played. He did not score every shot he took.

But he did LEARN every time, he developed from feedback and he continued trying. That is how he became the greatest!

Together, we will work on developing your mindset so that, step by step, you will learn about how to achieve any goal you wish ... and conquer anything life throws at you. Remember to work through to the end of the book and open your mind!

"The journey of a thousand miles begins with one step."

Lao Tzu
ancient Chinese philosopher and writer

How this book can help you

This book will help you to learn about your mind and how to train your mind so that you grow in every way. It will also give you an excellent chance to stop and think about YOU!

Yes, you, because you are the most important person in your world.

This book will equip you with appreciation for yourself and gratitude for the value that you bring to the world. And a passion for learning more about yourself and growing your mind and skills every day forever!

Every day you grow physically, and you are fully aware of that growth when you look back at your height chart or pictures to see how much you have grown.

Every day you also grow mentally and emotionally too. But that can be harder to measure or see. So at the end of this book, you can practice journaling, which will help your connection and reflection skills.

Do you remember that we call it the Game of Life?

Well, imagine yourself as the key player in that game and we are your coach throughout the book!

Use this book to reflect and write down what you are thinking, how you are feeling, what you have learnt about yourself and how you plan to improve your game.

You can do this!

Introducing Sticky

Hello,

I'm Sticky and I've been through some sticky situations in life! I've learnt that having a growth mindset helps to achieve things in life.

So I've got some great activities in this book to help you develop your mindset. You'll love it!

Enjoy!

Sticky will help you

Sticky will guide you through the activities in this book. He will encourage you to think, reflect and grow.

For some activities, you may want to speak with an adult too or reflect with someone who knows you well.

The activities are designed to get you thinking and help you develop life skills which will be important for all the different situations that life brings. The more life skills you have in your toolbox, the better equipped you will be! So get stuck in!

You can also use this book as part of your well-being journey so that you grow and understand more about yourself, to help you develop your mindset.

Read   Think   Practice   Grow

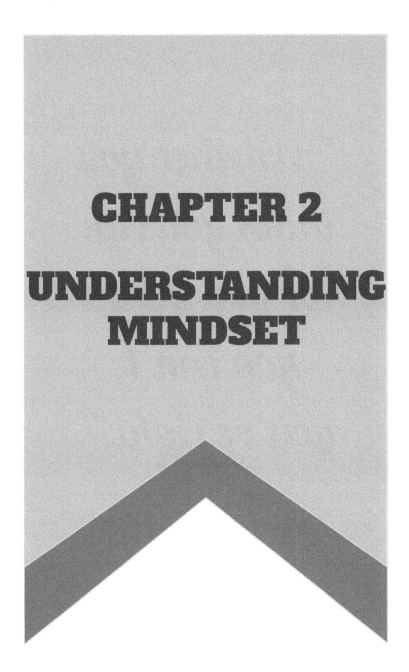

CHAPTER 2

UNDERSTANDING MINDSET

"Whether you think you can or you think you can't, you're right."

Henry Ford
American business magnate
and founder of the Ford Motor Company

What is mindset?

Mindset is your most powerful life tool!

It is like your secret weapon. Let's explain why...
Your mindset is your beliefs which shape how you view the world and yourself. It influences the way you think, feel and behave in any given situation. Therefore, it is true that what you think will impact your success or failure.

So, as Henry Ford said: "Whether you think you can or you think you can't, you're right."

Your mindset is the foundation of the outcome. It develops overtime and it can be moulded over days, weeks, months or even years. It develops from your thinking and, the best thing is, you have full control over it!

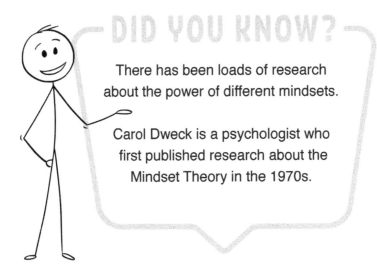

DID YOU KNOW?

There has been loads of research about the power of different mindsets.

Carol Dweck is a psychologist who first published research about the Mindset Theory in the 1970s.

Carol Dweck did research on students and found that there were two types of mindset. Some students had a fixed mindset and some had a growth mindset.

The research looked at each student's mindset towards their own intelligence. She found that students with a fixed mindset believed that intelligence is not changeable. They believed that if they couldn't do something then, that it was fixed and they would never be able do it.

However, the students with a GROWTH mindset believed that intelligence is MALLEABLE. They believed that if they couldn't do something YET, they would learn and grow until they could do it.

You can develop a GROWTH mindset by training your brain. This means that you will have a SUPER POWER growth mindset, which will motivate you to achieve everything you wish!

There are two main types of mindset:

 Fixed Mindset

 Growth Mindset

A Fixed Mindset is negative state of mind. It is when somebody believes that they cannot achieve something or that what they are able to achieve and their abilities are limited. Therefore, this person has limited progress and cannot grow.

Negative thoughts and negative self-talk can really hinder your confidence. People with a fixed mindset think, "I can't do that," or "That person is so good, but I'm rubbish." Thoughts like this are known as 'self-limiting beliefs' because they literally result in you limiting your success.

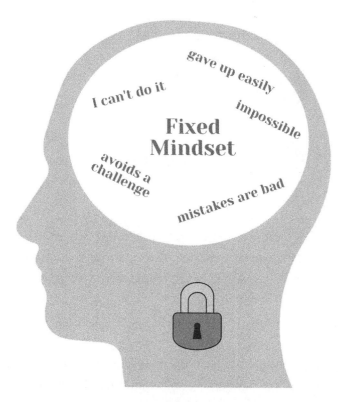

Write about a time when you had negative Fixed Mindset thoughts which held you back in something.

For example : I thought I would never swim; it grew into a fear of swimming because I kept saying to myself, 'I can't swim' so it really held me back.

A Growth Mindset is a positive state of mind where people believe that change, improvement and accomplishment will come through learning and practice.

People who have a growth mindset are always ready to take on new challenges and are open to learning.

They recognise that there is no such thing as failure or 'impossible', because every experience in life is a learning opportunity.

With this belief system, anything is possible! People with a growth mindset think, "I can do it!" or "I will try and persevere."

You should have a growth mindset to help grow your confidence and to enjoy your Game of Life!

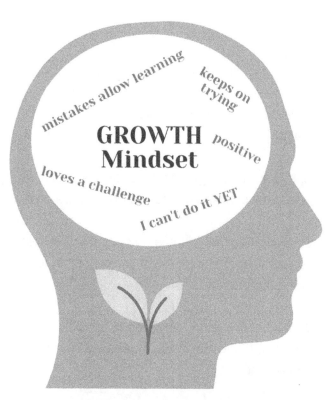

Write about a time when you had positive Growth Mindset thoughts which helped you to achieve something.

For example : I learnt to play snooker; I kept on trying and I realised that it's okay to miss a shot (or ten!) because each time I missed, I improved my technique!

You can start developing your growth mindset TODAY! Right NOW in fact!

It is well worth starting now, because when you have a growth mindset you will be more positive, you will feel more confident and ultimately it will improve your whole trajectory in life.

For most people, it can take time to practice a growth mindset. But for some people, it can be like flicking a switch and suddenly, with their new growth mindset, their whole outlook on life becomes more positive. Either way is perfectly normal.

The key thing is that what you can achieve in life with a growth mindset is limitless!

Your mind is...

your most powerful tool

Fun Quiz!

What are the 2 different types of mindset?

....

....

What is the name of the psychologist who first published research about the Mindset Theory?

....

Can you develop a Growth Mindset?

☐ Yes   ☐ No

REFLECTION

Tell Sticky two things which you
have learnt from this chapter

1...
....
....
2...
....
....

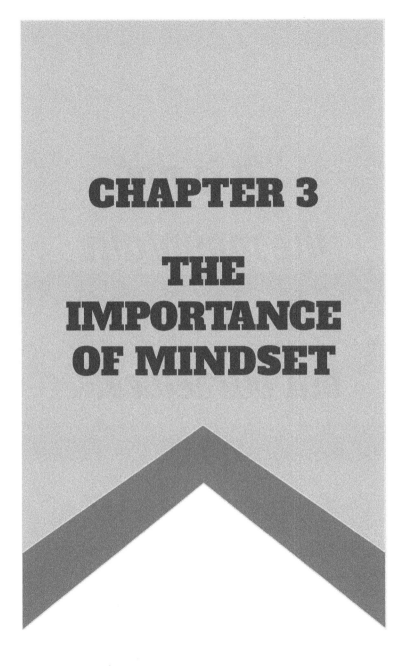

CHAPTER 3

THE IMPORTANCE OF MINDSET

"It is not the mountain we conquer but ourselves."

Sir Edmund Hillary
first man to conquer Everest

Why mindset matters

Your mindset controls the way you think, feel and behave in any given situation. So, clearly, it is powerful.

Training your mindset will make it even more powerful and will make you unstoppable.

Your mindset influences your thought patterns.

It influences how you learn new skills.

It influences how you see yourself.

It influences how you interact with the world.

It influences your achievements and successes in life.

It influences everything.

Everyone is in control of their own mind. So you are in control of your own thoughts and beliefs and ultimately your mindset. See? You are powerful!

Once you start exploring how powerful your mindset is, you will discover that you can break through any self-limiting belief (a thought or feeling that has the largest impact on holding you back) and realise that you can do anything!

Your mindset will help you to take on every challenge in life.

With a growth mindset, you will feel ready for every experience in life; you will move forward with opportunities and relationships. You will build yourself and grow. You will navigate your journey through life with courage and positivity. You will love yourself, embrace new challenges and achieve your goals. You will live life how you dream to!

Try the following quiz to see if your mindset sits more towards the fixed or growth mindset side at the moment.

Most importantly, remember, your amazing, malleable, magnificent brain can be moulded towards a GROWTH mindset. This book will help you to achieve that. So if you are struggling with a fixed mindset at the moment, do not feel disheartened because many people feel the same as you. Gradually they practice shifting and flipping their thoughts so they develop a growth mindset. (Sticky will help you to do this!)

YOU are in control of your powerful mind.

Your growth mindset will
be developed overtime
and is a skill which you will master.

a. READ the statement

b. DECIDE if you strongly agree/agree/ disagree/strongly disagree with the statement

c. CIRCLE the number in the column which you have picked

	STRONGLY AGREE	AGREE	DISAGREE	STRONGLY DISAGREE
My intelligence is something that I can't change much	0	1	2	3
It does not matter how much intelligence I have, I can always change it	3	2	1	0
Only a few people will be really good at sports, because you have to be born with that ability	0	1	2	3
I will be better at something if I work more on it	3	2	1	0
I often feel angry or upset when I get feedback about my performance	0	1	2	3
Truly smart people do not need to try hard	0	1	2	3

36

	STRONGLY AGREE	AGREE	DISAGREE	STRONGLY DISAGREE
People can challenge how intelligent they are	3	2	1	0
I appreciate when people, parents, teachers or coaches give me feedback about my performance	3	2	1	0
I am a certain kind of person and there is not much that I can do to change that	0	1	2	3
I enjoy learning new things	3	2	1	0

Adapted from the work of Carol Dweck

SCORE

22 - 30 = strong growth mindset
17 - 21 = growth mindset with some fixed ideas
11 - 16 = fixed mindset with some growth ideas
0 - 10 = strong fixed mindset

My score is ....

My current mindset is

....

37

YOUR TOMORROW....

STARTS TODAY

So start developing your growth mindset today and grow.

This will also help you to develop your life skills toolbox.

Your future self will thank you for it!

The impact of different mindsets

Your mindset influences your thoughts and beliefs on everything. This will impact your PERSPECTIVE on many different things, for example, football, Maths and life in general!

Perspective is the way that you look at something. For example, you can look at something from a positive point of view (growth mindset) or a negative point of view (fixed mindset).

Would you say this glass is half full? Or would you say this glass is half empty?

Sticky would say it is half full because he now has a positive perspective on things due to his growth mindset. But Sticky used to have a negative perspective on things when he had a fixed mindset.

Sticky has changed his way of thinking because he knows that his mind is powerful and that he controls his thoughts and actions.

Sticky's (Previous) Negative perspective. FIXED MINDSET	Sticky's (NOW) Positive perspective. GROWTH MINDSET

Oh no! I missed the goal...	I missed the goal this time... It's okay...
Everyone's laughing at me... I'm terrible at football...	It's only a game of football... I'll aim better next time...
Everyone thinks I'm rubbish...	I'll practice and improve my skills...
I'm useless and worthless!	I can do it!

Have a go…

Write a list of things that you have a negative perspective on the left-hand side of a piece of paper or notebook, then see if you can **FLIP** that thought to be a positive perspective on the right-hand side.

NEGATIVE perspective   **FLIP**   **POSITIVE** perspective

For example: I'm rubbish at Maths!

For example: I can improve my Maths skills by doing three extra questions every day – I just need a bit more practice.

REFLECTION

Tell Sticky three things which you
have learnt from this chapter

1...

....

2...

....

3...

....

CHAPTER 4

CONQUER YOUR MINDSET

"Conquer your mind, conquer your life."

Wesam Fawzi
growth and leadership performance strategist

To change and conquer your mindset is going to take some practice. So, let's going…!

Remember, step by step, we can do this.

So use our SEVEN step M.I.N.D.S.E.T method to support your journey and develop a GROWTH Mindset.

7

steps to conquer your mindset

The
M.I.N.D.S.E.T
method

M - Me

I - Inner world

N - New thinking

D - Daily affirmation

S - See success

E - Emotions

T - Transform

M – Me

You and your mind are powerful!

Your mind is like a super powerful computer.

All computers have programming which helps them to function. In a similar way, you have learnt things over the years (like your programming) which help you to function.

But sometimes the programming is not the correct programming for what we need. So understanding yourself is the first step towards retraining or resetting your mindset programming.

Knowing yourself, your skills and all the things you can do are a great way to start thinking about mindset.

Start by reflecting. This will help you to understand yourself better. Gradually you will start to value yourself. You will recognise who you are and accept all the qualities you already have.

Have a go at the next activities and really reflect on YOU!

Understanding yourself

Did you know that nobody, absolutely nobody, in the whole world is perfect? Read that again.
Nobody in the world is perfect.

BUT, we are all PERFECTLY UNIQUE.

Everyone has qualities which makes them special, different and uniquely perfect at being who they are.

Being different, thinking differently and being YOU-nique is a good thing.

Write all your skills, everything that you are good at and things which make you unique and perfectly 'you' here.

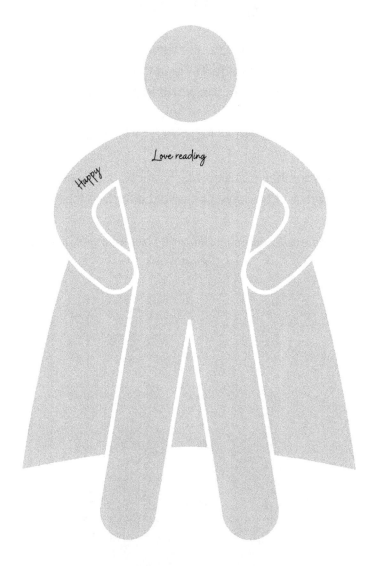

Embrace yourself and your uniqueness!

It is very important to understand yourself because you need to become your own best friend!

You need to love yourself, respect yourself and be happy in your own skin.

Everyone is different and that is what makes our world so special. Even if you had a twin brother or sister, he or she would still be very different to you.

There are some things which you are good at and other things which you are not so good at. That is normal. Just imagine if everyone was good at the same thing, such as swimming, and everyone wanted to become a lifeguard? Well… we would have no tennis players, no nurses, no vets, no shopkeepers, no football players, no singers…!

Being 'different' is a good thing! Everyone is unique and everyone brings something positive to this world. Once you see the uniqueness in yourself, then it becomes easier to embrace that and help your mind to grow.

Be your own best friend! Take the Best Friend Quiz!

What do I enjoy doing?

_____

_____

_____

What games or music do I enjoy?

_____

_____

_____

Which people do I love spending time with?

_____

_____

_____

What are the things that make me laugh or cheer me up?

_____

_____

_____

_____

What things do I not enjoy doing?

_____

_____

_____

_____

What situations or things make me feel unsure?

_____

_____

_____

_____

What things do I avoid?

_____

_____

_____

What is my biggest worry?

_____

_____

How do I react to problems or difficult situations?

_____

_____

_____

_____

The beauty of this world is that everyone is different but perfect in their own way. So remember to look for and embrace the uniqueness in others and in you.

It does not matter how old you are, you are the expert in being YOU. You know everything there is to know about you and you have full control over your own thoughts and feelings.

Most importantly, you have full control over your mindset.

So read on through the next letters of the M.I.N.D.S.E.T method to conquer your mindset.

M - Me

I - Inner world

N - New thinking

D - Daily affirmation

S - See success

E - Emotions

T - Transform

I – Inner world

To help develop your mindset, you need to think about what things influence you.

These could be:

a. EXTERNAL factors such as the outside world. For example, weather, other people, the news, social media, war, politics… the list goes on. These are things which can influence people to feel sad, jealous, worried, angry or upset. But the problem is that you have no control over these external factors. So NEVER let them impact you or influence your mindset.

b. INTERNAL factors such as your own thoughts, feelings and values. You should think of these as your INNER world. This is your safe space and sanctuary which you, and only you, have FULL CONTROL over.

So make your inner world positive, reflective, grateful, understanding and fulfilled.

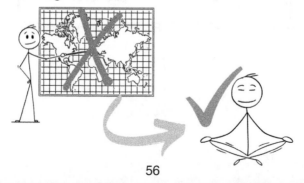

Valuable me

You are valuable.

Your thoughts, your beliefs, your actions are all valuable.
You may have heard people talk about 'values' like
honesty, resilience, compassion.

Have you ever stopped to think about what makes you,
you? What are your core values?

Well – now is your chance.

Sticky will help you out…

My VALUES…
Wisdom
Gratitude
Confidence

DID YOU KNOW?

Values are your important beliefs which guide or motivate your actions.

What are values?

Values are inside you and a part of you. They are your important beliefs. Your values will guide or motivate your actions.

Gratitude

Sticky believes in being grateful because life is a miracle and so he lives a life of gratitude. For example, he is grateful for being here in this moment, the people around him, feeling safe sitting at his desk… the list could go on.

Your values and actions are important because they make you who you are and will determine where you go and what you do in situations or life.

Using this list, think about and reflect on what each value means to you. Choose your three core values and write them in this box.

Adventure	Gratitude	Optimism
Authority	Growth	Peace
Balance	Happiness	Reputation
Challenge	Honesty	Resilience
Community	Influence	Respect
Confidence	Justice	Responsibility
Creativity	Kindness	Security
Curiosity	Knowledge	Stability
Determination	Leadership	Success
Fairness	Learning	Trust
Faith	Love	Wisdom

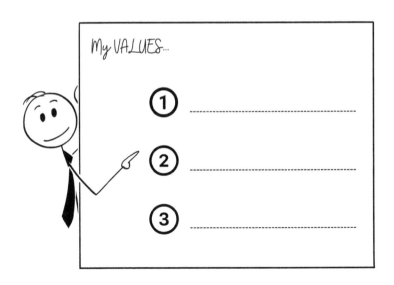

My VALUES...

1 --------------------------------

2 --------------------------------

3 --------------------------------

Believe

In your inner world, it is all about YOU.

Believing in yourself is essential.

Sometime the things we say to ourselves can hold us back.

For example: I'm not so good at organisation yet, so an action to help me get better with my organisation skills is to write a timetable and to...

These are examples of really important life skills which you will develop throughout life.

Have a look at these and pick one that you are already good at and write about why you are good at it.

For example: I'm good at independence because I walk to school safely every day.

_____

_____

Now pick one that you are not so good at yet, then write two actions which you can take to get a bit better at it.

For example: I'm not so good at organisation yet, so an action to help me get better with my organisation skills is to write a timetable and to...

_____

_____

_____

_____

_____

_____

Delete it

Many people have a few negative thoughts floating around in their brain and mind. Don't panic, that's okay. BUT you must never amplify them or allow them to impact you and your confidence.

A useful way to deal with this is to DELETE these thoughts when you spot something negative in your mind.

Write down some thoughts which you want to get rid of on a piece of paper. Then, simply put the paper straight into the bin so the thoughts are released from your mind.

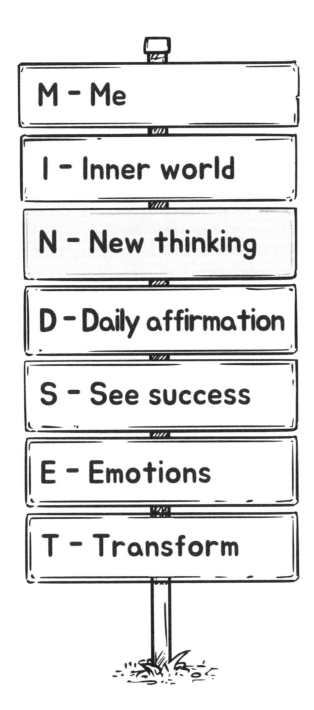

N – New thinking

It is very important to understand your thoughts and feelings. Your mindset is determined by your thoughts. Negative thoughts will breed a negative mindset; whereas positive thoughts will encourage a positive growth mindset.

We like to use the analogy of a cake. The cake can represent you, and the ingredients you put into the cake will determine the outcome of the cake, how much it rises (or not) and how it looks.

Start thinking about what ingredients must go into your cake for you to start building your confidence. Words like KINDNESS, TRUST or GRATITUDE are important ingredients in your cake.

They are examples of essential ingredients which must go into your cake, because they are POSITIVE. Your cake must have positive or good ingredients going into it so that it rises well, is balanced and has a uniqueness to it which nobody else can remake.

Everybody knows that there are ingredients which are essential for a cake and some ingredients which should be avoided. For example, if you do not put in any self-raising flour, then your cake will be flat, unbalanced and not reach its full potential of being a big, bright, delicious cake, despite all the other ingredients that you add.

Write all the ingredients you want to put into your cake here.

For example: Confidence

As you can see, tier by tier, you can start building up your cake. In the same way, you can use the right ingredients to build up each area of your life to build a fully empowered and confident you.

All of those things you have listed are POSITIVE ingredients which will be good for your cake.

It is equally important to talk about and discuss which ingredients could be NEGATIVE and damage your cake.

Write anywhere around the sign below all the negative ingredients which you should avoid putting into your cake!

For example :Self-doubt

All of these ingredients or negative factors will have a negative impact on your cake. This analogy helps us to understand the thoughts and feelings which you must NOT keep in inside you. This will help you to flourish and grow!

You are a
DIAMOND

Do you know how diamonds are made?

We won't give you a science lesson here, but basically, diamonds are formed from rock after high pressure under the Earth's surface. Due to high heat and pressure, the carbon atoms bond together and form a tough diamond.

In a similar way, as humans, our minds can become tougher when under pressure. Therefore, we can grow as a better person and shine, despite a setback or intense pressure.

Write about a time when you have been under pressure.

For example: I felt under pressure when I was the Captain of the football team as I had never done that before and I wanted to impress my friends...

What life skills did you learn?

For example: As a football captain, I learnt life skills such as organisation because I had to get my school work done as well as train with my team. I also learnt communication skills because...

How do those skills help your confidence and help you SHINE?

For example: I learnt better communication skills being a football captain which now helps me feel more confident when talking to other people. I feel happy now that I can shine and speak to loads of different people.

It is helpful to spot confidence in yourself and in others. You can learn so much from confident role models around you. We can also understand and support someone when they are not so confident. This will help us to become better people.

Write down how you behave or react when you are feeling low in confidence. Remember, it is really useful for you to spot these behaviours and reactions so that you can make changes early when you are feeling low in confidence.

For example: When I feel low in confidence, I sit by myself and will not get involved in something, in case I can't do it.

It can be tricky to talk or think about a tough or stressful time when you felt low in confidence. BUT it's so important to reflect and think of positive ways of dealing with that situation.

M – Me

I – Inner world

N – New thinking

D – Daily affirmation

S – See success

E – Emotions

T – Transform

D – Daily affirmation

Affirmations are positive statements which can boost you and encourage a positive mindset.

If repeated on a daily basis, affirmations will reinforce your positive new thinking and help you to feel empowered, so your affirmations can motivate, inspire and encourage you to take action and reach your goals.

For example, affirmations can be statements like:

I love myself for who I am.

I believe in myself and my dreams.

My challenges are my opportunities.

I am beautiful just as I am.

I create my own happiness.

As you can see, affirmations build optimism and stop negative self-talk. This is crucial when you are developing a resilient, optimistic, growth mindset.

Before you think of your affirmations, reflect and write down which life skills you ALREADY have.

For example: I can plan my day which means I have organisational skills.

_____

_____

_____

_____

_____

_____

_____

_____

Once you start thinking about it, there are a lot! Be proud of all the life skills which you already have.

Perhaps we should start calling a it a Life Skills Suitcase!

Now think forward. Think into the future and think about which life skills you will need in the next few years ahead. List them here.

Keep this list safe because you will need to look back over this later on in the book and also in later years down the line.

For example: I need more independence skills so that I can walk to school.

When thinking forward or thinking about the future, close your eyes and think BIG.

Imagine yourself as whatever you want to be and wherever you want to be.

Think big now so that you can start your growth mindset journey today. Because, day by day, and step by step, you will become that big person.

We want you to love and enjoy the journey to becoming big. Yes, you will grow physically bigger, but the growth of your mind is the most valuable growth.

So keep feeding your mind with positivity and endless love so that you are emotionally bigger with an unstoppable mindset.

The power of your name

On the next page, you are going to make an acrostic poem about YOU-nique you using your name!

Your name is valuable.

Your name is a powerful connection to your identity. It will have deep personal, family based or cultural connections.

DID YOU KNOW?

Some people say that
there are TWO meanings to your name.

1 - The name you are GIVEN at birth

2 - The name you EARN in life

Be proud of your name. But also earn yourself a good name by doing good things in life and do your name proud.

Write out each letter of your name in capital letters vertically down the left side of the frame. Then write your acrostic poem with each line starting with the letters in your beautiful name. Think of powerful, fun, motivating words which help to describe you.

Channel your energy

Affirmations work because when you say them every day, you create a shift in your energy.

The energy and positivity in your affirmations spreads within you.

You then put that energy and positivity out into the Universe by your thoughts, feelings and actions.

Then, by the Law of Attraction and the Law of Vibration, more positivity is attracted to you.

CAUTION – if you put out negative energy into the Universe, guess what you attract back? Correct, more negative things! So focus on being positive and seeing more positivity in what you do, then more positivity will come back to you.

Write your affirmations down

Your affirmations will help you to feel empowered, energised and eager to achieve by reinforcing your growth mindset.

So here are some tips to help you write your affirmations.

Personal

Positive

Present

Your affirmations must be PERSONAL and relate to you, your thoughts, your feelings and your goals. Many affirmations start with "I am…" because this helps you to focus on keeping them personal to you.

Your affirmations must be written from a POSITIVE perspective. So do not use words such as not, won't, don't or can't. For example, write 'I am brave' instead of 'I am not scared'. This is because your mind will miss the 'not' and will only hear 'I am scared' and focus on the negativity of it.

Your affirmations must be in the PRESENT tense. This is so that you hear it as already being true. For example, you already have achieved the goal you aimed for. This will then energise you more and make you achieve it.

Over to you… write your affirmations here. Keep them safe and repeat them to yourself every day.

My affirmations

For example: Life is good. I appreciate my life. My life is what I make it.

M – Me

I – Inner world

N – New thinking

D – Daily affirmation

S – See success

E – Emotions

T – Transform

S – Success

This is also known as VISUALISATION… but there is no V in mindset so it is called See Success!

Seeing or visualising your success is essential to help you achieve it.

Visualisation is to picture what you want to achieve in the future as if it were true today.

It involves seeing as the strongest sense. And, when you add visualisation to hearing your positive affirmations from the previous step, then you massively increase your success rate.

So get into the good habit of visualising your goals every day and saying your positive affirmations daily too. Or perhaps even twice a day as part of your daily routine.

This regular reminder will keep your conscious and subconscious mind aware of your goals and your mind will see and seize opportunities to achieve your goals.

Visualisation is powerful for your mindset because your mind is already trained to know that thought comes before action.

So your thoughts are supporting the actions that you want and reinforcing the goals that you will achieve.

How to get the best results with visualisation

There are two types of visualisation:

1. OUTCOME visualisation (see the end goal)
2. PROCESS visualisation (see every step to the end goal)

When you use both types together, then you get to the goal quicker.

For example, if your goal is to get onto the sports team, then visualise your outcome of being on the team, but also visualise the process of you at the training sessions, playing well and scoring goals.

Visualisation can be used for lots of other aims too, such as reducing anxiety, improving your performance in a subject and being able to speak in front of people.

There are six key steps to practice visualisation…

1. Write down what you want in detail. Think about all five senses as you describe what you want and how it will make you feel.

2. Add more details as your vision develops and gradually you will be able to feel and experience having achieved your goal. This will motivate you more!

3. Imagine the feelings and emotions that you attach to the outcome of your vision. Visualisation of the outcome will make you more likely to achieve it.

4. Take action every day – small steps – towards achieving your vision.

5. Expand your knowledge and challenge yourself further to reach your next level vision.

6. Every day for at least five minutes, reflect and look at everything you have achieved.

Every small win counts (like making your bed, smiling at the shopkeeper, holding the door open for a stranger, saying please and thank you).

All of these small wins make you a better human being. So remember the basics and grow from there to the stars!

Vision board

A vision board is pictures and words of your dreams and goals to help you visualise them so that you achieve them.

Making a vision board helps by taking the thoughts and goals out of your head and making them physically real in front of you.

The overall aim of a vision board is to help you:

- identify and clarify your goals
- reinforce your daily affirmations
- maintain focus on your goals

Your vision board could be digital or physical – it is your choice. The pictures you use could come from magazines, newspapers, printed from the internet, your photo album, anywhere you choose.

Some people like to have sections to their vision board such as family, education, spiritual, social, fitness. But there are no strict rules for your vision board.

It is about you, your goals and your dreams.

So stop reading for a moment. Close your eyes. Now start thinking about what you want to put on your vision board.

Use these three questions to help make your vision board:

1. WHO do you want to be in life? Define the person you want to be and how it relates to your chosen vision.

2. WHERE do you want to be in life? Think about where you want to life.

3. WHAT experiences do you want to have in life?

My vision board

Sticky's Vision Board

M – Me

I – Inner world

N – New thinking

D – Daily affirmation

S – See success

E – Emotions

T – Transform

Emotions

Emotions come from inside you.

Emotions can be positive or negative. They can influence your thoughts and actions. Some emotions can trigger such an intense response in your body that it feels overwhelming to have that emotion.

For example, anger makes some people breath deeper, get hotter and shout. Or anxiety gives some people a fast heartbeat, causes them to sweat become red, and have a dry mouth.

This can be worrying for the person having that emotion and also for the person who is seeing that emotion.

So it is best to deal with emotions sensibly and with logic.

TOP TIPS

How to manage your emotions

1. Identify the emotion

2. Talk about and explain the emotion

3. Suggest how to make things better or who to talk to

Say what you feel

Being able to describe your emotions and how they make you feel is really helpful. This is because it will encourage you with the next step of managing that emotion and the feeling which it triggers inside you.

Here are some descriptions which you could use to describe how you or others are feeling.

 Overjoyed, Delighted, Elated, Energetic, Lively, Boisterous, Silly, Excited

 Content, Happy, Pleased, Positive, Proud, Relaxed, Relieved, Glad, Satisfied, Calm

 Miserable, Tired, Shy, Confused, Down, Stressed, Hurt, Embarrassed, Empty, Disappointed

 Worried, Upset, Anxious, Alarmed, Lonely, Sad, Scared, Nervous, Ashamed, Regretful, Grief-stricken, Hopeless

 Furious, Devastated, Angry, Mad, Fuming, Annoyed, Agitated, Cross, Frustrated

Reflect and write about a time when you felt ANGRY or SAD by something?

For example: When Mummy threw my toy in the bin
because I bashed my brother with it, I felt...

Draw a picture of how it made you feel and behave.

How did that emotion go away?

For example: When I talked to Mummy, I realised that I
should have not bashed anyone with my toy and I said
sorry...

Reflect and write about a time when you felt HAPPY or BOISTEROUS about something?

For example: At my friend's birthday party...

_____

_____

_____

Draw a picture of how it made you feel and behave.

How did that emotion go away?

For example: I became tired out in the end and needed to

have a rest...

_____

_____

_____

Sticky's stuck – can you help him?

Sticky just got picked on in the playground by some older kids. They kicked the football at him, were nasty about how he looked and teased him, calling him a loner.

Look at Sticky below. Which words would you use to describe his emotions?

Within a few moments, Sticky's emotions have changed. Describe his emotions now.

What advice would you give Sticky to help him control his emotions?

_____

_____

_____

_____

_____

_____

Who would you suggest that he talks to for help with this situation?

_____

_____

_____

_____

_____

_____

keep
CALM
& be
KIND

There are lots of ways that you can channel your emotions so that you can turn any negative emotion into a positive emotion. Here are a few examples:

 Play or listen to music

 Play in the garden or go for a walk

 Sit quietly for a moment or meditate

 Do some sport or other activity

 Learn some deep-breathing exercises

 Yoga

Do one of these, or a combination of them. It will always help you to channel away those moments of negative energy during an emotional time. Once you release the negative energy, then it will allow positive energy to flow.

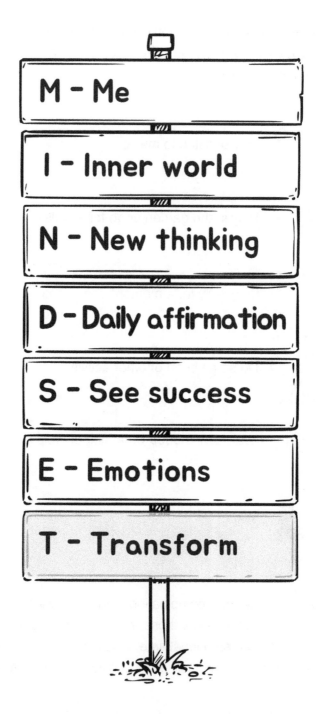

T – Transform

Get started TODAY!

And over the next few days, weeks and months, you will notice a difference in your way of thinking, your well-being, your mood, your perspective of life… your MINDSET. You will feel more happy and content.

You will want to hang out with new people, expand your circle of friends, enjoy new interactions and grow as YOU. You will want to take on new challenges and you will not fear failure, because you know that you will never fail – you will simply learn and grow.

You will have confidence and certainty in your ability to walk alone if needed, or opposite to the crowd to do what is right for you.

You have it inside you to be a leader and not a follower. This book is a stepping stone for you to enter into the world of self-care and self-development.

Remember that the mindset changes you are making will be with you forever. You are the EXPERT of being YOU. Be the master of your MINDSET!

Goal setting

As part of your transformation, you will be regularly setting yourself goals. And we believe in you. You will achieve your goals!

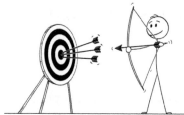

You have learnt valuable techniques, such as positive affirmations and visualisation, which will be excellent tools in your life.

These techniques can also be used when goal setting.

The first cog in your mind in goal setting is to have a clear picture in your mind about exactly WHAT the goal is. This involves visualisation.

The second cog in your mind is to breakdown the goal so that you have a PLAN of HOW you are going to achieve that goal.

The third cog in your mind is the IMPACT of WHY achieving this goal is so important to you. In fact, this cog is THE most important because it is the cog which MOTIVATES you. Your motivation is actually the secret sauce which keeps all the cogs turning.

Cog 1 in your mind when goal setting = the clear goal image.

It looks at WHAT your goal is. You need to be very specific so that you are giving a very clear instruction to your mind and body of exactly what you are trying to achieve.

Your mind will then set off working to find a solution for HOW (cog 2) you will achieve that goal.

To help you be specific about your goal, you should set SMART goals. This stands for:

Specific

Measurable

Achievable

Realistic

Time frame

Cog 2 in your mind when goal setting = the Plan.

It looks at HOW your goal is going to be achieved.

Again, you need to be very specific with the plan. Start with the end in mind.

Your mind will then set off visualising that goal which will feed into the WHY (cog 3) and that will keep you motivated to achieve your goal (even on days when you don't feel like it!).

IMPACT (WHY)

3

Cog 3 in your mind when goal setting = the Impact.

It looks at WHY your goal is so important to you.

It will keep you motivated to achieve your goal because it is the reason why you have a clear goal (cog 1) and have developed a plan of how to achieve it (cog 2).

The impact and satisfaction or celebration you will feel once you achieve that goal is the important driving force here.

Use your five senses so that you are able to feel every part of the success in achieving your goal.

My goals

By each cog, write down the details of what, how and why for one of your goals.

CLEAR GOAL IMAGE (WHAT)
1

PLAN (HOW)
2

IMPACT (WHY)
3

Fun quiz

What are the SEVEN steps to conquer your mindset?

....

....

....

....

....

....

....

Believe in Yourself

List two actions which you will take
to improve your mindset

"Every winner was once a beginner."

Daniel Priestley
author and international speaker

CHAPTER 5

EVERYDAY MINDSET

Your mindset in new situations

Remember that your mind is powerful.

Your mindset is controlled by YOU!

So knowing, loving and conquering your unique self is very important.

In new situations, there are so many external factors which are different. For example, when you move class at school each year. Or when you join a new extra-curricular club. Or if you move from one town to another.

But remember to focus on what is within your control and use the most powerful tool you have – your mind – to overcome any challenges. You should continue to develop your internal or inner world so that you can rely on yourself.

All of these situations will require you to know yourself and trust yourself and have a growth mindset!

M.I.N.D.S.E.T
for life

The method which you have learnt to conquer your mindset will help you develop a growth mindset and, importantly, an unstoppable mindset!

Life will sometimes have ups and downs with some lefts and rights too.

But you will be unshakable and unstoppable if you continue to apply what you have learnt.

Do I need a TOOLBOX?

(Not one with screwdrivers and a hammer in it!)

What you do need is this 'Life Skills Toolbox' – this is a metaphorical toolbox!

It will contain many important life skills which you have already been collecting over the years. But there are lots more to add to it.

For example, so far, you will already have some basic communication skills in there – such as how to negotiate being able to stay up late on a Friday night or having a sleepover, or survival skills such as pouring milk on your cornflakes every morning and flushing the toilet! These 'life skills' are important. But there are some more advanced life skills which you need to add.

Life skills are like the 'nuts and bolts' of what you need to know. They are the lessons you learn from living in today's world, from the interactions that you have with people and what you learn about yourself along the way. Here is a list of some life skills which we have recently learnt:

- how to cope with different emotions
- conflict resolution skills
- how to check the oil in a car (with an adult)

And the list goes on! But you will only spot these skills when you are on the lookout for them. So a good habit is to reflect on your day and reflect on the learning or experiences you have gained.

Time management   Self-care

Coping with pressure

Money management

Organisation

Positive thinking

LIFE SKILLS

Communication skills

Building healthy
relationships

Citizenship

Independence

Big picture thinking

Your vision focuses on tomorrow or the future, and what you want to become or achieve.

Your mission focuses on today or now, and what you do in order to make progress and accomplish your vision.

It is important to think about both, because you can't work on without the other. Think about it; you will only reach your vision if you have a mission focusing you on getting there.

Remember we spoke about values earlier?

Well, those values are what will drive you while you are on your mission to achieve your vision.

Here is Sticky to help you understand all three points together.

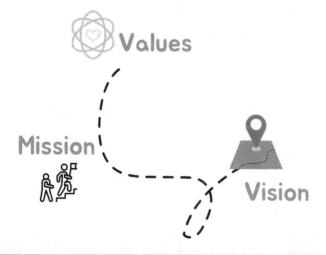

Sticky will help you think about this more. His values are WISDOM, GRATITUDE and CONFIDENCE.

His values guide and motivate his actions, like his interaction with the people and world around him.

When Sticky was younger, his Vision was to be Sports Captain. He was on a Mission to overcome any obstacle to achieve his Vision.

He encountered may obstacles along the way; feeling he was not good enough at sport, jealous friends teasing him or putting him down, giving up his free time for sports training.

However, he addressed each obstacle using his guiding values. His wisdom helped him understand and foresee that the fruit of his efforts would come later. His wisdom also helped him understand the negative feelings of jealousy coming from those around him. His value of gratitude helped him to be thankful for his sporty skills and feel positive. His value of confidence helped him to address his internal worries of sometime feeling unsure and to face and deal with each setback. And, finally, he achieved his vision!

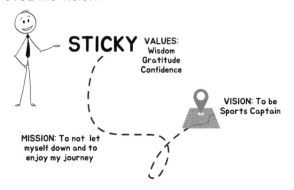

STICKY VALUES: Wisdom Gratitude Confidence

VISION: To be Sports Captain

MISSION: To not let myself down and to enjoy my journey

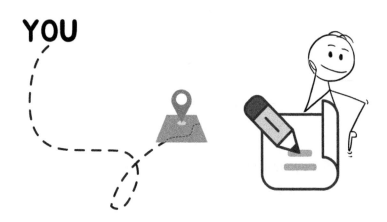

YOU

Do you have a goal you want to achieve? (It can be big or small.)

Write it down as your Vision and then write down your Mission.

Think about your Values again and how they will help you to reach your Vision.

_____

_____

_____

_____

_____

_____

_____

_____

_____

REFLECTION

Tell Sticky three things which you
have learnt from this chapter

1..
....
2..
....
3..
....

List two actions which you will take
to achieve your vision

1

2

CHAPTER 6

MINDSET JOURNAL

"Journal writing is a voyage to the interior."

Christina Baldwin
best-selling author on personal growth

Your time to shine in the 'Game of Life'

Wow, what a journey you have been on! You have learnt about mindset and how to take control to conquer your mindset.

The techniques that you have worked on and developed through the activities in this book will help you every day.

Now it is your time to keep practising everything which you have learnt from this book, especially the M.I.N.D.S.E.T method.

For the next 30 days, journal your progress every day. This will strengthen what you have learnt and help you practice your everyday mindset techniques.

Keep this book safe as a resource or diary, and reflect back on it so you can see your growth mindset journey. You will be amazed by the transformation over time!

Please do just one thing in return for us…

ENJOY YOUR GAME OF LIFE!

FIVE MINUTE JOURNALING

_____

_____

_____

_____

_____

_____

_____

MY POSITIVE AFFIRMATIONS

....

....

....

....

TOP THREE THINGS ABOUT TODAY

○ _____

○ _____

○ _____

EMOTIONS I FELT TODAY

MY RATING OF TODAY

MY MEMORIES FROM TODAY

LIFE SKILLS FOR MY TOOLBOX

_____

_____

_____

_____

TODAY I FELT INSPIRED BY:

WHAT I WISH TO DO TOMORROW

FIVE MINUTE JOURNALING

_____

_____

_____

_____

_____

_____

_____

MY POSITIVE AFFIRMATIONS

....

....

....

....

TOP THREE THINGS ABOUT TODAY

O _____

O _____

O _____

_____

EMOTIONS I FELT TODAY

MY RATING OF TODAY

MY MEMORIES FROM TODAY

....

....

LIFE SKILLS FOR MY TOOLBOX

_____

_____

_____

_____

TODAY I FELT INSPIRED BY:

....

....

....

....

WHAT I WISH TO DO TOMORROW

....

....

....

....

....

....

FIVE MINUTE JOURNALING

_____
_____
_____
_____
_____
_____
_____

MY POSITIVE AFFIRMATIONS

....
....
....
....

TOP THREE THINGS ABOUT TODAY

○ _____

○ _____

○ _____

EMOTIONS I FELT TODAY

MY RATING OF TODAY

MY MEMORIES FROM TODAY

....
....

LIFE SKILLS FOR MY TOOLBOX

_____
_____
_____
_____

TODAY I FELT INSPIRED BY:

....
....
....
....

WHAT I WISH TO DO TOMORROW

....
....
....
....
....
....
....

FIVE MINUTE JOURNALING

_____
_____
_____
_____
_____
_____
_____

MY POSITIVE AFFIRMATIONS

....
....
....
....

TOP THREE THINGS ABOUT TODAY

○ _____

○ _____

○ _____

EMOTIONS I FELT TODAY

MY RATING OF TODAY

MY MEMORIES FROM TODAY

....
....

LIFE SKILLS FOR MY TOOLBOX

_____
_____
_____
_____

TODAY I FELT INSPIRED BY:

....
....
....
....

WHAT I WISH TO DO TOMORROW

....
....
....
....
....
....
....

FIVE MINUTE JOURNALING

_____

_____

_____

_____

_____

_____

_____

MY POSITIVE AFFIRMATIONS

....

....

....

....

TOP THREE THINGS ABOUT TODAY

O _____

O _____

O _____

EMOTIONS I FELT TODAY

MY RATING OF TODAY

MY MEMORIES FROM TODAY

....

....

LIFE SKILLS FOR MY TOOLBOX

_____

_____

_____

_____

TODAY I FELT INSPIRED BY:

....

....

....

....

WHAT I WISH TO DO TOMORROW

....

....

....

....

....

....

FIVE MINUTE JOURNALING

_____

_____

_____

_____

_____

_____

_____

MY POSITIVE AFFIRMATIONS

....

....

....

....

TOP THREE THINGS ABOUT TODAY

○ _____

○ _____

○ _____

_____

EMOTIONS I FELT TODAY

😄 🙂 😐 🙁 😢 😭

MY RATING OF TODAY

☆ ☆ ☆ ☆ ☆

MY MEMORIES FROM TODAY

....

....

LIFE SKILLS FOR MY TOOLBOX

_____

_____

_____

_____

TODAY I FELT INSPIRED BY:

....

....

....

....

WHAT I WISH TO DO TOMORROW

....

....

....

....

....

....

FIVE MINUTE JOURNALING

_____
_____
_____
_____
_____
_____
_____

MY POSITIVE AFFIRMATIONS

LIFE SKILLS FOR MY TOOLBOX

_____
_____
_____
_____

TOP THREE THINGS ABOUT TODAY

○ _____

○ _____

○ _____

TODAY I FELT INSPIRED BY:

WHAT I WISH TO DO TOMORROW

EMOTIONS I FELT TODAY

MY RATING OF TODAY

MY MEMORIES FROM TODAY

FIVE MINUTE JOURNALING

_____

_____

_____

_____

_____

_____

_____

MY POSITIVE AFFIRMATIONS

LIFE SKILLS FOR MY TOOLBOX

_____

_____

_____

_____

TOP THREE THINGS ABOUT TODAY

○ _____

○ _____

○ _____

TODAY I FELT INSPIRED BY:

WHAT I WISH TO DO TOMORROW

EMOTIONS I FELT TODAY

MY RATING OF TODAY

MY MEMORIES FROM TODAY

FIVE MINUTE JOURNALING

_____

_____

_____

_____

_____

_____

_____

MY POSITIVE AFFIRMATIONS

....

....

....

....

TOP THREE THINGS ABOUT TODAY

○ _____

○ _____

○ _____

EMOTIONS I FELT TODAY

MY RATING OF TODAY

MY MEMORIES FROM TODAY

....

....

LIFE SKILLS FOR MY TOOLBOX

_____

_____

_____

_____

TODAY I FELT INSPIRED BY:

....

....

....

....

WHAT I WISH TO DO TOMORROW

....

....

....

....

....

....

FIVE MINUTE JOURNALING

_____

_____

_____

_____

_____

_____

_____

MY POSITIVE AFFIRMATIONS

....

....

....

....

TOP THREE THINGS ABOUT TODAY

O _____

_____

O _____

_____

O _____

_____

EMOTIONS I FELT TODAY

MY RATING OF TODAY

MY MEMORIES FROM TODAY

....

....

LIFE SKILLS FOR MY TOOLBOX

_____

_____

_____

_____

TODAY I FELT INSPIRED BY:

....

....

....

....

WHAT I WISH TO DO TOMORROW

....

....

....

....

....

....

FIVE MINUTE JOURNALING

_____

_____

_____

_____

_____

_____

_____

MY POSITIVE AFFIRMATIONS

....

....

....

....

TOP THREE THINGS ABOUT TODAY

O _____

O _____

O _____

_____

EMOTIONS I FELT TODAY

MY RATING OF TODAY

MY MEMORIES FROM TODAY

....

....

LIFE SKILLS FOR MY TOOLBOX

_____

_____

_____

_____

TODAY I FELT INSPIRED BY:

....

....

....

....

WHAT I WISH TO DO TOMORROW

....

....

....

....

....

....

FIVE MINUTE JOURNALING

_____

_____

_____

_____

_____

_____

_____

MY POSITIVE AFFIRMATIONS

....

....

....

....

TOP THREE THINGS ABOUT TODAY

○ _____

○ _____

○ _____

_____

EMOTIONS I FELT TODAY

MY RATING OF TODAY

☆ ☆ ☆ ☆ ☆

MY MEMORIES FROM TODAY

....

....

LIFE SKILLS FOR MY TOOLBOX

_____

_____

_____

_____

TODAY I FELT INSPIRED BY:

....

....

....

....

WHAT I WISH TO DO TOMORROW

....

....

....

....

....

....

....

FIVE MINUTE JOURNALING

_____

_____

_____

_____

_____

_____

_____

MY POSITIVE AFFIRMATIONS

....

....

....

....

TOP THREE THINGS ABOUT TODAY

○ _____

_____

○ _____

_____

○ _____

_____

EMOTIONS I FELT TODAY

MY RATING OF TODAY

MY MEMORIES FROM TODAY

....

....

LIFE SKILLS FOR MY TOOLBOX

_____

_____

_____

_____

TODAY I FELT INSPIRED BY:

....

....

....

....

WHAT I WISH TO DO TOMORROW

....

....

....

....

....

....

....

FIVE MINUTE JOURNALING

_____

_____

_____

_____

_____

_____

_____

MY POSITIVE AFFIRMATIONS

LIFE SKILLS FOR MY TOOLBOX

_____

_____

_____

_____

TOP THREE THINGS ABOUT TODAY

○ _____

○ _____

○ _____

_____

TODAY I FELT INSPIRED BY:

WHAT I WISH TO DO TOMORROW

EMOTIONS I FELT TODAY

MY RATING OF TODAY

MY MEMORIES FROM TODAY

FIVE MINUTE JOURNALING

_____

_____

_____

_____

_____

_____

_____

MY POSITIVE AFFIRMATIONS

....

....

....

....

TOP THREE THINGS ABOUT TODAY

○ _____

○ _____

○ _____

_____

EMOTIONS I FELT TODAY

MY RATING OF TODAY

MY MEMORIES FROM TODAY

....

....

LIFE SKILLS FOR MY TOOLBOX

_____

_____

_____

_____

TODAY I FELT INSPIRED BY:

....

....

....

....

WHAT I WISH TO DO TOMORROW

....

....

....

....

....

....

FIVE MINUTE JOURNALING

_____

_____

_____

_____

_____

_____

_____

MY POSITIVE AFFIRMATIONS

LIFE SKILLS FOR MY TOOLBOX

_____

_____

_____

_____

TOP THREE THINGS ABOUT TODAY

○ _____

○ _____

○ _____

_____

TODAY I FELT INSPIRED BY:

WHAT I WISH TO DO TOMORROW

EMOTIONS I FELT TODAY

MY RATING OF TODAY

MY MEMORIES FROM TODAY

FIVE MINUTE JOURNALING

_____

_____

_____

_____

_____

_____

_____

MY POSITIVE AFFIRMATIONS

....

....

....

....

TOP THREE THINGS ABOUT TODAY

○ _____

○ _____

○ _____

EMOTIONS I FELT TODAY

MY RATING OF TODAY

LIFE SKILLS FOR MY TOOLBOX

_____

_____

_____

_____

TODAY I FELT INSPIRED BY:

....

....

....

....

WHAT I WISH TO DO TOMORROW

....

....

....

....

....

....

MY MEMORIES FROM TODAY

....

....

FIVE MINUTE JOURNALING

_____

_____

_____

_____

_____

_____

_____

MY POSITIVE AFFIRMATIONS

....

....

....

....

TOP THREE THINGS ABOUT TODAY

○ _____

○ _____

○ _____

EMOTIONS I FELT TODAY

MY RATING OF TODAY

MY MEMORIES FROM TODAY

....

....

LIFE SKILLS FOR MY TOOLBOX

_____

_____

_____

_____

TODAY I FELT INSPIRED BY:

....

....

....

....

WHAT I WISH TO DO TOMORROW

....

....

....

....

....

....

FIVE MINUTE JOURNALING

_____
_____
_____
_____
_____
_____
_____

MY POSITIVE AFFIRMATIONS

....
....
....
....

TOP THREE THINGS ABOUT TODAY

○ _____

○ _____

○ _____

EMOTIONS I FELT TODAY

😄 🙂 😐 🙁 ☹️ 😭

MY RATING OF TODAY

☆ ☆ ☆ ☆ ☆

MY MEMORIES FROM TODAY

....
....

LIFE SKILLS FOR MY TOOLBOX

_____
_____
_____
_____

TODAY I FELT INSPIRED BY:

....
....
....
....

WHAT I WISH TO DO TOMORROW

....
....
....
....
....
....

FIVE MINUTE JOURNALING

_____

_____

_____

_____

_____

_____

_____

MY POSITIVE AFFIRMATIONS

....

....

....

....

TOP THREE THINGS ABOUT TODAY

O _____

O _____

O _____

EMOTIONS I FELT TODAY

MY RATING OF TODAY

MY MEMORIES FROM TODAY

....

....

LIFE SKILLS FOR MY TOOLBOX

_____

_____

_____

_____

TODAY I FELT INSPIRED BY:

....

....

....

....

WHAT I WISH TO DO TOMORROW

....

....

....

....

....

....

FIVE MINUTE JOURNALING

_____
_____
_____
_____
_____
_____
_____

MY POSITIVE AFFIRMATIONS

....
....
....
....

TOP THREE THINGS ABOUT TODAY

○ _____

○ _____

○ _____

EMOTIONS I FELT TODAY

MY RATING OF TODAY

MY MEMORIES FROM TODAY

....
....

LIFE SKILLS FOR MY TOOLBOX

_____
_____
_____
_____

TODAY I FELT INSPIRED BY:

....
....
....
....

WHAT I WISH TO DO TOMORROW

....
....
....
....
....
....
....

FIVE MINUTE JOURNALING

_____

_____

_____

_____

_____

_____

_____

MY POSITIVE AFFIRMATIONS

LIFE SKILLS FOR MY TOOLBOX

_____

_____

_____

_____

TOP THREE THINGS ABOUT TODAY

○ _____

○ _____

○ _____

TODAY I FELT INSPIRED BY:

WHAT I WISH TO DO TOMORROW

EMOTIONS I FELT TODAY

MY RATING OF TODAY

☆ ☆ ☆ ☆ ☆

MY MEMORIES FROM TODAY

FIVE MINUTE JOURNALING

_____

_____

_____

_____

_____

_____

_____

MY POSITIVE AFFIRMATIONS

LIFE SKILLS FOR MY TOOLBOX

_____

_____

_____

_____

TOP THREE THINGS ABOUT TODAY

O _____

O _____

O _____

_____

TODAY I FELT INSPIRED BY:

EMOTIONS I FELT TODAY

WHAT I WISH TO DO TOMORROW

MY RATING OF TODAY

MY MEMORIES FROM TODAY

FIVE MINUTE JOURNALING

_____

_____

_____

_____

_____

_____

MY POSITIVE AFFIRMATIONS

LIFE SKILLS FOR MY TOOLBOX

_____

_____

_____

_____

TOP THREE THINGS ABOUT TODAY

○ _____

○ _____

○ _____

TODAY I FELT INSPIRED BY:

WHAT I WISH TO DO TOMORROW

EMOTIONS I FELT TODAY

MY RATING OF TODAY

☆ ☆ ☆ ☆ ☆

MY MEMORIES FROM TODAY

FIVE MINUTE JOURNALING

_____
_____
_____
_____
_____
_____
_____

MY POSITIVE AFFIRMATIONS

....
....
....
....

TOP THREE THINGS ABOUT TODAY

○ _____

○ _____

○ _____

EMOTIONS I FELT TODAY

😀 😊 😐 🙁 😞 😩

MY RATING OF TODAY

☆ ☆ ☆ ☆ ☆

MY MEMORIES FROM TODAY

....
....

LIFE SKILLS FOR MY TOOLBOX

_____
_____
_____
_____

TODAY I FELT INSPIRED BY:

....
....
....
....

WHAT I WISH TO DO TOMORROW

....
....
....
....
....
....
....

FIVE MINUTE JOURNALING

_____

_____

_____

_____

_____

_____

_____

MY POSITIVE AFFIRMATIONS

LIFE SKILLS FOR MY TOOLBOX

_____

_____

_____

_____

TOP THREE THINGS ABOUT TODAY

○ _____

○ _____

○ _____

_____

TODAY I FELT INSPIRED BY:

EMOTIONS I FELT TODAY

MY RATING OF TODAY

WHAT I WISH TO DO TOMORROW

MY MEMORIES FROM TODAY

FIVE MINUTE JOURNALING

_____
_____
_____
_____
_____
_____
_____

MY POSITIVE AFFIRMATIONS

....
....
....
....

TOP THREE THINGS ABOUT TODAY

○ _____

○ _____

○ _____

EMOTIONS I FELT TODAY

MY RATING OF TODAY

MY MEMORIES FROM TODAY

....
....

LIFE SKILLS FOR MY TOOLBOX

_____
_____
_____
_____

TODAY I FELT INSPIRED BY:

....
....
....
....

WHAT I WISH TO DO TOMORROW

....
....
....
....
....
....
....

FIVE MINUTE JOURNALING

_____
_____
_____
_____
_____
_____
_____

MY POSITIVE AFFIRMATIONS

....
....
....
....

TOP THREE THINGS ABOUT TODAY

O _____

O _____

O _____

_____

EMOTIONS I FELT TODAY

MY RATING OF TODAY

☆ ☆ ☆ ☆ ☆

MY MEMORIES FROM TODAY

....
....

LIFE SKILLS FOR MY TOOLBOX

_____
_____
_____
_____

TODAY I FELT INSPIRED BY:

....
....
....
....

WHAT I WISH TO DO TOMORROW

....
....
....
....
....
....

FIVE MINUTE JOURNALING

_____

_____

_____

_____

_____

_____

_____

MY POSITIVE AFFIRMATIONS

....

....

....

....

TOP THREE THINGS ABOUT TODAY

○ _____

○ _____

○ _____

_____

EMOTIONS I FELT TODAY

MY RATING OF TODAY

MY MEMORIES FROM TODAY

....

....

LIFE SKILLS FOR MY TOOLBOX

_____

_____

_____

_____

TODAY I FELT INSPIRED BY:

....

....

....

....

WHAT I WISH TO DO TOMORROW

....

....

....

....

....

....

FIVE MINUTE JOURNALING

_____

_____

_____

_____

_____

_____

_____

MY POSITIVE AFFIRMATIONS

....

....

....

....

TOP THREE THINGS ABOUT TODAY

○ _____

○ _____

○ _____

_____

EMOTIONS I FELT TODAY

😀 🙂 😐 🙁 😞 😖

MY RATING OF TODAY

☆ ☆ ☆ ☆ ☆

MY MEMORIES FROM TODAY

....

....

LIFE SKILLS FOR MY TOOLBOX

_____

_____

_____

_____

TODAY I FELT INSPIRED BY:

....

....

....

....

WHAT I WISH TO DO TOMORROW

....

....

....

....

....

....

"Keep growing every day!"

Onkaar & Avneet

CERTIFICATE OF ACHIEVEMENT

EVERYDAY MINDSET AWARDS

• •

for completing their Mindset Journey

Onkaar

Onkaar
Author

Avneet

Avneet
Author